SCIENCE
NEWS for
KIDS

Earth Science

SCIENCE NEWS for **KIDS**

Computers and Technology

Earth Science

The Environment

Food and Nutrition

Health and Medicine

Space and Astronomy

SCIENCE NEWS for KIDS

Earth Science

Series Editor
Tara Koellhoffer

With a Foreword by
Emily Sohn,
Science News for Kids

CHELSEA CLUBHOUSE
An Imprint of Chelsea House Publishers

Earth Science

Copyright © 2006 by Infobase Publishing

Chelsea Clubhouse
An imprint of Chelsea House Publishers
132 West 31st Street
New York NY 10001

For Library of Congress Cataloging-in-Publication Data, please contact the publisher.

ISBN 0-7910-9124-4

Text and cover design by Takeshi Takahashi
Layout by Ladybug Editorial & Design

Printed in the United States of America

Bang   10 9 8 7 6 5 4 3 2 1

This book is printed on acid-free paper.

Contents Overview

Detailed Table of Contents

Detailed Table of Contents

by Emily Sohn
Science News for Kids

Science, for many kids, is just another subject in school. You may have biology tests and astronomy quizzes to study for, chemistry formulas to memorize, physics problems to work through, or current events to report on. All of it, after a while, can seem like a major drag.

Now, forget about all that, and think about your day. What did you eat for breakfast? How did you get to school and what did you think about along the way? What makes the room bright enough for you to see this book? How does the room stay cool or warm enough for you to be comfortable? What do you like to do for fun?

All of your answers, in some way, involve science. Food, transportation, electricity, toys, video games, animals, plants, your brain, the rest of your body: Behind the scenes of nearly anything you can think of, there are scientists trying to figure out how it works, how it came to be, or how to make it better. Science can explain why pizza and chocolate taste good. Science gives airplanes a lift. And science is behind the medicines that make your aches and pains go away. Most exciting of all, science never stands still.

Science News for Kids tracks the trends and delves into the discoveries that make life more interesting and more efficient every day. The stories in these volumes explore a tiny fraction of the grand scope of research happening around the world. These stories point out the questions that push scientists to probe ever deeper into physics, chemistry, biology, psychology, and more. Reading about the challenges of science will spark in you the same sort of curiosity that drives researchers to keep searching for answers, despite setbacks and failed experiments. The stories here may even inspire you to seek out your own solutions to the world's puzzles.

Being a scientist is hard work, but it can be one of the best jobs around. You may picture scientists always tinkering away in their labs, pouring chemicals into flasks and reading technical papers. Well, they do those things some of the time. But they also get to dig around in the dirt, blow things up, and even ride rockets into outer space. They travel around the world. They save lives. And, they get to spend most of their time thinking about the things that fascinate them most, all in the name of work.

Sometimes, researchers have revelations that change the way we think about the universe. Albert Einstein, for one, explained light, space, time, and other aspects of the physical world in radically new terms. He's perhaps the most famous scientist in history, thanks to his theories of relativity and other ideas. Likewise, James Watson and

Francis Crick forever changed the face of medicine when they first described the structure of the genetic material DNA in 1953. Today, doctors use information about DNA to explain why some people are likely to develop certain diseases and why others may have trouble reading or doing math. Police investigators rely on DNA to solve mysteries when they analyze hairs, blood, saliva, and remains at the scene of a crime. And scientists are now eagerly pursuing potential uses of DNA to cure cancer and other diseases.

Science can be about persistence and courage as much as it is about grand ideas. Society doesn't always welcome new ideas. Before Galileo Galilei became one of the first people to point a telescope at the sky in the early 1600s, for example, nearly everyone believed that the planets revolved around Earth. Galileo discovered four moons orbiting Jupiter. He saw that Venus has phases, like the moon. And he noticed spots on the sun and lumps on the moon's craggy face. All of these observations shook up the widely held view that the heavens were perfect, orderly, and centered on Earth. Galileo's ideas were so controversial, in fact, that he was forced to deny them to save his life. Even then, he was sentenced to imprisonment in his own home.

Since Galileo's time, the public has so completely accepted his views of the universe that space missions have been named after him, as have craters on the moon and on Mars. In 1969, Neil Armstrong became the first person to stand on the moon. Now, astronauts spend months in orbit, living on an international space station, floating in weightlessness. Spacecraft have landed on planets and moons as far away as Saturn. One probe recently slammed into a comet to collect information. With powerful telescopes, astronomers continue to spot undiscovered moons in our solar system, planets orbiting stars in other parts of our galaxy, and evidence of the strange behavior of black holes. New technologies continue to push the limits of what we can detect in outer space and what we know about how the universe formed.

Here on Earth, computer technology has transformed society in a short period of time. The first electronic digital computers, which appeared in the 1940s, took up entire rooms and weighed thousands of pounds. Decades passed before people started using their own PCs (personal computers) at home. Laptops came even later.

These days, it's hard to imagine life without computers. They track restaurant orders. They help stores process credit cards. They allow you to play video games, send e-mails and instant messages to your friends, and write reports that you can edit and print without ever picking up a pen. Doctors use computers to diagnose their patients, and banks use computers to keep track of our money. As computers become more and more popular, they continue to get smaller, more powerful, less expensive, and more integrated into our lives in ways we don't even notice.

Probes that fly to Pluto and computers the size of peas are major advances that don't happen overnight. Science is a process of small steps, and a new discovery often starts with a single question. Why, for example, do hurricanes and tsunamis form? What is it like at the center of Earth? Why do some types of french fries taste better than others? Research projects can also begin with observations. There are fewer tigers in India than there used to be, for instance. Kids now weigh more than they did a generation ago. Mars shows signs that the planet once supported life.

The next step is investigation, which can take on many forms, depending on the subject. Brain researchers, for one, often do experiments in their laboratories with the help of sophisticated equipment. In one type of neuroscience study, subjects repeatedly solve tasks while machines measure activity in their brains. Some environmental scientists who study climate, on the other hand, collect data by tracking weather patterns over the years. Paleontologists dig deep into the earth to look for clues about what the world was like when dinosaurs were alive. Anthropologists learn about other cultures by talking to people and collecting stories. Doctors monitor large numbers of patients taking a new drug or no drug to figure out whether a drug is safe and effective before others can use it.

Designing studies requires creativity, and scientists spend many years training to use the tools of their profession. Physicists need to learn complicated mathematical formulas. Ecologists make models that simulate interactions between species. Physicians learn the name of every bone and blood vessel in the body. The most basic tools, however, are ones that everyone has: our senses. The best way to start learning about the world through science is to pay attention to what you smell, taste, see, hear, and feel. Notice. Ask questions. Collect data. Do experiments. Draw tentative conclusions. Ask more questions.

Most importantly, leave no stone unturned. There's no limit to the topics available for research. Robots, computers, and new technologies in medicine are the waves of the future. Just as important, however, are studies of the past. Figuring out what Earth's climate used to be like and which animals and plants used to live here are the first steps toward understanding how the planet is changing and what those changes might mean for our future. And don't forget to look around at what's going on around you, right now. You might just be surprised at how many subjects you can find to investigate.

Ready to get started? The stories in this book are great sources of inspiration. Each of the articles comes directly from the *Science News for Kids* Website, which you can find online at *http://sciencenewsforkids.org*. All articles at the site, which is updated weekly, cover current events in science, and all are written with middle-school students in mind. If anything you read in this book sparks your interest, feel free to visit the Website to check out the latest developments and find out more.

And keep an eye out for an occasional feature called "News Detective." These essays describe what it's like to be a science journalist, roaming the world in search of scientists at work. Science writing is an often-overlooked career possibility, but science writers have endless opportunities to learn about many things at once, to share in the excitement of scientific discovery, and to help scientists get the word out about the significance of their work.

So, go ahead and turn the page. There's so much left to discover.

Section 1

Weather and Climate

From devastating hurricanes like Katrina, which hit New Orleans and the U.S. Gulf Coast in late August 2005, to the ongoing threat of global warming, weather has taken center stage in the daily news—and not just because people want to know what to wear when they leave the house. Changing weather patterns affect more than just the temperature and how much rain or snow we get. Over the long term, a change in climate can dramatically alter the kinds of plants farmers can grow and which species of animals can survive in certain places. In this section, we explore some of the most important aspects of weather and climate and how they affect your everyday life and the world as a whole.

The first article examines the phenomenon of hurricanes, from how they form over warm waters to the way their winds and fierce rains can damage and even destroy entire cities.

Have you ever felt like you have to suffer through school when the weather is warm and beautiful, just to have rain or snow ruin your weekend plans? The second article in this section poses an interesting question: Is the weather on weekends different from the weather during the school and work week?

The third article addresses an issue of long-term global importance: the warming of the Earth's climate. Everyone has heard about the danger of global warming, but not everybody is familiar with the very real threats this possibility poses, which writer Emily Sohn explains.

The final article in this section looks at the terrible problem of drought—a prolonged lack of rainfall that leads to severe water shortages that make it hard for plants—and even people—to survive.

—The Editor

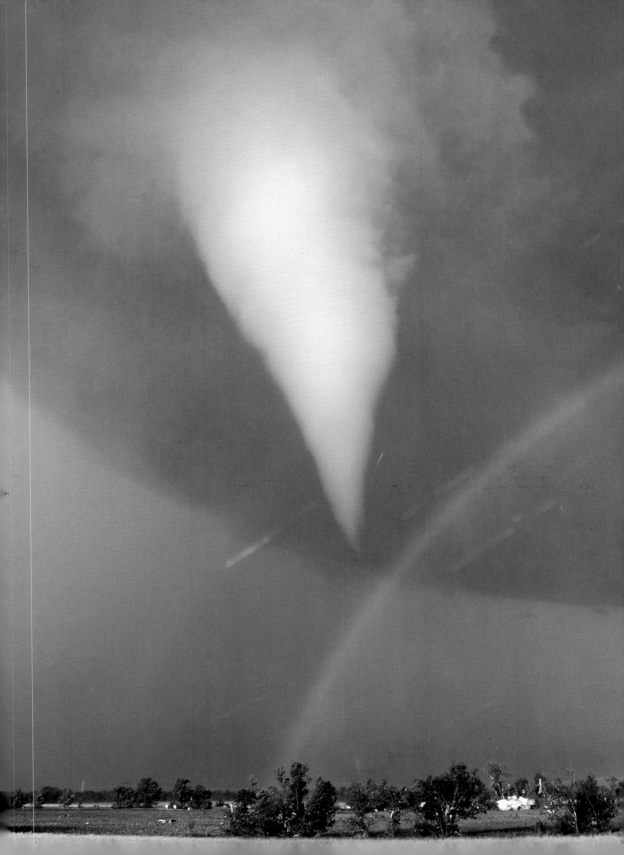

Horrific Hurricanes

The official "hurricane season" in the Atlantic Ocean takes place between June 1 and November 30 each year. Most of the worst storms occur in late summer and through the fall, as evidenced by some of the most devastating hurricanes in recent memory: Wilma, which hit Florida in October 2005; and Katrina, which hit Louisiana and the Gulf Coast in late August 2005, causing billions of dollars' worth of damage and leaving the usually thriving city of New Orleans a virtual ghost town. What exactly is a hurricane? How do hurricanes form? Why are they so powerful? In the following article, author Emily Sohn answers these questions and many others.

Recipe for a Hurricane

by Emily Sohn

Before Reading:

- **What news have you heard lately about hurricanes?**

- **What resources do people have to find out about hurricanes?**

In August 2004, Charley ripped through Florida. The **hurricane** tore up trees, wiped out houses, and caused more than $7 billion in damage.

At about the same time, a series of **typhoons** killed at least 40 people in the Philippines and forced more than a million people to flee. Three weeks later, Hurricane Frances followed Charley's lead, again pummeling Florida—to the dismay of many people in the state. Then came Ivan and Jeanne. Hurricane Jeanne killed more than 1,000 people in Haiti, before heading for the Bahamas and Florida.

The onslaughts may have been massive, but they weren't a surprise.

Every year, major storms cause major problems around the world. There's nothing people can do to stop the powerful forces of nature. But new techniques are helping scientists to predict how, when, and where the big ones will occur. The more accurately scientists can give warnings, the more likely people are to grab their valuables and flee to safety.

Predictions are improving. "We've gotten better over the years, especially the last few years," says Phil Klotzback. He's an atmospheric scientist at Colorado State University in Fort Collins.

STORM FORMATION

There's plenty left to learn, though. Even when scientists can figure out where a storm is headed, winds can change at the last minute, carrying the storm in a new direction.

Charley, for example, was originally headed right for the city of Tampa Bay but ended up hitting the Florida coast further south.

"A little shift can make a big difference," says meteorologist Eric Blake. He works at the National Hurricane Center in Miami. "**Meteorology** is both a science and an art."

The science part depends mostly on computer simulations, or models, and knowledge of the past. Scientists have been collecting data about storms for decades. They've noticed patterns that suggest what it takes for a strong storm to form in the first place.

Hurricanes that hit the United States start when a thunderstorm forms off the coast of Africa. Storms also develop over tropical waters in other parts of the world. Most storms end up falling apart on their own, and we never hear about them.

For a hurricane to get organized, "conditions have to be just right," Klotzbach says.

First, the ocean water needs to be warm enough so that the winds can take up water through evaporation, which rises into the air. As it rises, the vapor cools and turns back into liquid. This process releases heat. The cycle of evaporation and condensation is like an engine that causes winds to swirl and grow. It drives the formation of a hurricane.

If wind speeds inside the swirling mass reach 40 miles [64 km] per hour, the system is classified as a "tropical storm," and it gets a name. At 75 miles [121 km] per hour, it becomes a hurricane. In the western Pacific, hurricanes are known as typhoons.

On average, 60 or 70 storms form off Africa every year, Klotzbach says. About 10 of them get names. There are usually about 6 hurricanes. Two tend to be very intense, with winds of 115 miles [185 km] per hour or higher.

- **How does a hurricane form?**

Hurricane season lasts from June 1 to November 30.

Ninety percent of all hurricanes hit in August, September, and October, Klotzbach says. Half usually happen in September, when conditions are most favorable.

HURRICANE TRACKS

- **When is hurricane season?**

The National Hurricane Center tracks storms as they happen. Observations and data come from people on ships out at sea and from satellites in orbit around Earth. Computers crunch the data for warning signs of a developing storm.

Years of observations have supplied scientists with fairly reliable patterns that help them figure out what's going to happen next.

In the Northern Hemisphere, hurricanes spin counter-clockwise around a center, called an eye (Figure 1.1). Tropical trade winds carry these systems across the ocean toward the southeastern United States.

When a big one starts to form, meteorologists begin to watch it closely. Some experts even fly into the eye to get a closer look. As the storm approaches land, meteorologists at the Hurricane Center send out advisories every six hours.

When they get to land, storms often turn north before cruising east again, back out to sea. But with unpredictable changes in temperature and wind patterns, it doesn't always work that way.

"Forecasts of the exact track have gotten considerably better over the last 10 years," Blake says. Still, such predictions are good for only a few hours. And storms are constantly full of surprises.

"Storms can track in all sorts of strange ways," Klotzbach says. Such quirks keep people glued to their

Figure 1.1 This weather map from the National Oceanic and Atmospheric Administration (NOAA) shows Hurricane Floyd, which ravaged the east coast of the United States in September 1999.

radios and TVs when hurricanes approach land, as they listen for the latest reports on which way a storm is headed.

FUTURE STORMS

As if that weren't tricky enough, researchers at Colorado State try to make predictions months ahead of time. Before the start of each hurricane season, they announce how many hurricanes and severe storms they expect will occur in the coming summer and fall.

Some years are more active than others. And knowing what to expect is important to lots of people, including emergency managers, insurance companies, and people who live on the coasts. Being prepared can save millions of dollars and lots of lives.

To predict the future, the Colorado State researchers use computer models to look to the past. "Basically, we see what global climate features worked well in forecasting previous years," Klotzbach says. "We assume the future is going to be like the past."

For instance, when temperatures at the surface of the Atlantic Ocean are warm in late spring and early summer, the hurricane season tends to be very active. In years that have a weather pattern called **El Niño**, on the other hand, high winds tend to break storms up, and few hurricanes develop.

Researchers at Colorado State have used such patterns to make predictions for the last 21 years, Klotzbach says. Their predictions are now a lot better than those they made even a few years ago.

In May 2004, for example, Klotzbach and his team predicted an "above-average" probability of hurricanes hitting the U.S. coast in the coming hurricane season. The researchers said they expected 14 named storms and eight hurricanes.

In fact, August 2004 had near-record storm activity, and September was also above average. The researchers expected October 2004 to be a little quieter than usual.

- **How do researchers at Colorado State University predict hurricanes?**

PERSONALITY

Although there are patterns as to when and where hurricanes occur, every hurricane is different. Each one has its own personality.

To acknowledge that variety, every big storm gets its own name. Storms in the Atlantic are named after people. In the Pacific, storms can be named after flowers or take on nicknames. The World Meteorological Organization decides names in advance, and the alphabetical list rotates every six years. Names on the list get replaced only if a storm with a particular name is especially severe—killing lots of people or costing loads of money. That way, the name takes its place in history.

• Why are these storms named?

Teddy. Sally. Emily. Dennis. The names may sound friendly. But, watch out. Hurricanes are like bullies. Even with a name like Debby or Charley, big storms can turn on you when you least expect it. Knowing what to look for can help you get out before it's too late.

After Reading:

- **Why do meteorologists classify storms?**

- **Look back at old newspapers from the summer of 2004 and compare Hurricane Charley and Hurricane Ivan. Where did they start? What were their courses? How were they reported on?**

- **Why do you think most storms form off the coast of Africa?**

- **Why can storms be unpredictable?**

- **Explain the difference between a tornado and a hurricane.**

- **How are computers used to understand hurricanes?**

Weekend Versus Weekday Weather

If you've ever looked wistfully out the window at school, staring at the bright sun and dreaming of the upcoming weekend, then been disappointed by torrential rains that kept you trapped in your house on your precious days off, then this article is for you. Writer Emily Sohn explores a recent study that suggests weekend weather actually *is* different from the weather we experience during the week—at least in certain places. Read more about this startling discovery.

—The Editor

Weekend Weather Really Is Different

by Emily Sohn

Do you ever feel like the weather is out to get you? All week long, it seems, you sit inside at school while the sun shines outside. Then, as soon as the weekend comes, the sky turns gray. There's rain in the forecast.

In some ways, you may be right. Weekend weather differs from weekday weather in certain places, say researchers who studied more than 40 years of weather data from around the world. They focused on temperature differences between daytime highs and nighttime lows. This difference measurement is called the **diurnal temperature range**, or DTR.

Part of the study involved 660 weather stations in the continental United States. At more than 230 of these sites, the average DTR for Saturday, Sunday, and Monday was different from the average DTR for Wednesday, Thursday, and Friday, the researchers found. The difference was small—only several tenths of a Celsius degree—but the pattern was striking enough to make the scientists take notice.

In the southwestern United States, temperature ranges were typically broader on weekends. In the Midwest,

14

weekdays saw larger daily temperature variations.

This sort of weekly rise and fall doesn't line up with any natural cycles, the researchers say. Instead, they blame human activities, possibly air pollution from those activities, for these weather effects. For example, tiny particles in the air could affect the amount of cloud cover, which would in turn affect daily temperatures.

So, tiny windborne particles from California, generated on weekdays, might first affect weather close to

What Weather?

Weather matters a great deal on Earth. People in the path of September 2003's Hurricane Isabel were asked to leave low-lying areas in case of flooding. Ships had to leave port and head for open water so they wouldn't be smashed against docks by the strong winds. Businesses were closed and precautions taken to save lives and property.

Does weather matter on other worlds as well? Of course! Saturn, for example, has storms that could cover the entire Earth. So science-fiction writers should always mention weather in order to write believable stories.

Or should they? Here's your challenge. Name at least three science-fiction settings where a story could occur without the writer needing to talk about any weather at all.

home in the southwest, then later influence midwestern weather.

It looks like your weekend weather has a lot do with which way the wind blows and where it comes from.

Going Deeper:

Perkins, Sid. "Weekend Weather Really Is Different." *Science News* **164 (October 11, 2003): 237–238. Available online at** *http://www.sciencenews.org/20031011/note13.asp*.

Global Warming Melts Earth's Ice

Once, the Earth was covered in ice, which made it hard for many forms of life to exist. But is today's climate too warm? As environmental scientists have been warning us for many years, the answer is probably "yes." According to new research, polar ice is melting faster than ever before, making the danger of rising seas a very real threat, as writer Emily Sohn explains in the following article.

—The Editor

Ice Age Melting and Rising Seas

by Emily Sohn

Most of us are used to seasons. Each year, spring follows winter, which follows autumn, which follows summer, which follows spring, with winters that are colder than summers. But Earth can go through much larger temperature cycles over longer times than those that we normally experience.

Between 65,000 and 35,000 years ago, for instance, the planet was much colder than it is now. The temperature also changed a lot during that time, with periods of warming and cooling. Ice melted during the warm periods, which made sea levels rise. Water refroze during the cold times.

A new study sheds light on where ice sheets melted during the ice age's warm periods. It now seems that the ice melted at both ends of Earth, rather than just in northern or southern regions. This result surprised the researchers, who are from the University of Bern in Switzerland.

Scientists have long assumed that most of the ice melting occurred in the Northern Hemisphere during the 30,000-year period of the ice age. That's because the North Pole is surrounded by land, while the South Pole is surrounded by the Antarctic Ocean. It's easier for ice sheets to flow and grow on land. Otherwise, the ice can just slip into the ocean instead of building up.

The researchers used a computer model to look at different types of melting that might affect sea level. They compared these results to evidence of how temperatures and currents actually changed during that time.

The model showed that melting just in the Northern Hemisphere would have shut down ocean currents and lowered sea temperatures much more than actually happened in the North Atlantic. Studies suggest that melting just in the Southern Hemisphere would have been impossible, too.

The only reasonable conclusion, the scientists decided, was that ice melted equally in the North and the South. The rest of the story about why this would occur, however, remains a mystery.

Going Deeper:

Perkins, Sid. "North and South: Equal Melting From Each Hemisphere Raised Ice Age Sea Levels." *Science News* **166 (August 28, 2004): 133. Available online at** *http://www.sciencenews.org/ articles/20040828/fob5.asp.*

The Danger of Drought

It's perfectly normal for most places on Earth to go through seasons that have less rain than other times of the year. However, when no rain falls at all for long periods of the time, that is not normal—and it can be extremely dangerous. Extended periods with less precipitation than usual are referred to as "droughts," and they are, unfortunately, all too common in parts of the world, particularly the American West and Southwest. You may think of water-bearing disasters, like hurricanes, as the bigger threat, but in many cases, a lack of water can be even more serious, especially over the long term, as writer Emily Sohn demonstrates in the following article.

—The Editor

A Dire Shortage of Water

by Emily Sohn

Before Reading:

- **In the United States, where are you most likely to experience a drought?**

If it were up to me, the weather would be hot and sunny every day.

Good thing it's not up to me. Earth needs rain and snow.

Without a reliable supply of water, we would have nothing to drink, nothing to sustain our crops. Swimming pools would be empty. Lawns would have no grass. Electricity would be expensive. Plants would die; animals would follow.

Such a water shortage may sound extreme, but it's happening right now in parts of the western United States. An area called the Colorado River Basin, which stretches from Wyoming to Arizona, is in the middle of the worst **drought** in at least 500 years (Figure 1.2). Rivers in this region are at their lowest levels ever recorded.

If the drought continues, the results could be disastrous. The river basin is a major source of water for big

Figure 1.2 Glen Canyon Dam in Arizona shows the signs of pro-longed drought. The reservoir of water it holds back is much lower than normal.

cities, including Las Vegas, Phoenix, and Los Angeles. Entire ecosystems depend on this water, as do ranchers and many other people who live and work in the area.

- Why is the Colorado River Basin vital to the lives of people living in the southwestern part of the United States?

EXTREME WEATHER

Extreme weather and natural disasters are a normal part of life on Earth. Tornadoes, floods, hurricanes, and earthquakes destroy houses and kill people. Droughts are also menacing. They can last for decades. No one knows how to predict or stop them. In fact, many things that people do make the problem worse.

Experts say that major droughts in the 1200s and 1300s may have driven the Native American Anasazi out of places such as Mesa Verde in Colorado and Chaco Canyon in New Mexico.

"Water is life," says geologist John Dohrenwend of Teasdale, Utah. "If you don't have it, the land can't support life."

Out West, rivers and flood plains make up just 3% of the land area, Dohrenwend says. But these 3% support a full 90% of the region's plant and animal life.

- **Compared to other types of natural disasters, what makes droughts particularly threatening?**

CAUSES

Scientists are just beginning to understand the conditions that lead to droughts. They're finding that small changes in the flow of wind and water can have a huge effect on climate around the globe.

Strangely enough, much of the story depends on the temperature of water in the oceans.

Normally, winds blow west across the tropical Pacific Ocean, away from Central and South America. As wind-driven warm water moves over the ocean, it piles up in Indonesia and elsewhere in the western Pacific. Warm air rises offshore, causing rain to fall. Meanwhile, cold water comes up from the bottom off the coast of South America. This flow allows a richness of life to flourish near the coast, and it helps maintain predictable weather patterns from season to season.

Every 5 to 10 years or so, though, the wind dies down. As a result, the surface of the Pacific Ocean gets warmer. Rainfall then tends to fall further to the east. Such a change in weather causes, among other things, floods in Peru and droughts in Australia and Indonesia. This new weather pattern is known as El Niño.

An opposite cascade of events happens during the weather pattern called **La Niña**, when Pacific surface temperatures cool down. Both El Niño and La Niña, when they happen, usually last for 2 to 4 years.

The current drought in the West could last much longer than that. In fact, historical records show that droughts typically go on for 10 to 50 years.

And it's not just El Niño and La Niña at work. In the last few years, scientists from the U.S. Geological Survey (USGS) have begun to link precipitation on the Colorado Plateau

- **How often does El Niño take place? How long does it last?**

- **What is the difference between El Niño and La Niña?**

to temperature shifts both in the Pacific Ocean and in the Atlantic Ocean.

ATLANTIC EFFECTS

A recent statistical study by USGS researchers found that less moisture falls on the United States when surface temperatures in the North Atlantic are warmer than normal. These conditions prevailed during a number of droughts over the past century.

The study also found a correlation between warm water in the central North Pacific and drought in the southwestern and northern plains of the United States. When water is warm in both the North Atlantic and the North Pacific at the same time, conditions can get mighty dry in the American West.

This explains at least a part of what's going on right now in the Colorado River Basin, Dohrenwend says.

- **Why does warm water in both the North Atlantic and the North Pacific produce droughts in the southwestern United States?**

Records show that the basin's annual flow volume has been dropping for more than a century. But the drought has grown much worse since the year 2000. Compared to measurements taken in 1922, water flow has dropped to one-third of its original rate.

PEOPLE PROBLEMS

Oceans can't take all of the blame for the impact of today's drought, Dohrenwend says.

Although ocean temperatures may be an important factor in starting a drought, people are making the problem of water shortages much worse. Dohrenwend notes that cities are growing faster in the Southwest than anywhere else in the country. And people keep pouring in.

"Many of these people are retired persons who lived in the northeast or northwest and want to get out of the cold," Dohrenwend says. It's hard for them to adjust to using less water than they're used to, he adds, and they don't want to let go of their golf courses, green lawns, or long showers.

"Over time, more and more water has to be allocated to people moving in and less goes to everything else," Dohrenwend says.

Ironically, as the drought continues, the cycle feeds on itself. Ranchers go out of business because they don't have enough water to grow alfalfa for their cattle. Then, developers arrive and build more homes. As more people move in, the demand for water continues to grow—even as the supply of water rapidly dwindles.

HOW LONG?

It's impossible to know how long this drought will last,

and some scientists are beginning to fear the worst.

Dohrenwend, for one, has been monitoring the Lake Powell reservoir, a huge water-storage site in southern Utah. The reservoir provides drinking water to the area. It also feeds into the Glen Canyon Dam, which has huge turbines to generate enormous amounts of electricity.

• **How are people in the south-western United States contributing to the effects of the drought that is taking place in the Colorado River Basin?**

Right now, water levels in the reservoir are 115 feet [35 meters] below full, Dohrenwend says.

The shallower the lake gets, the more stagnant it becomes. The water has less oxygen in it, and chemicals from agricultural waste become more concentrated. Eventually, the water would become too toxic to drink.

Dohrenwend has been using photographs and measurements to document the movement of sediment through rivers toward the Lake Powell reservoir. Ever since the drought began, his research shows, piles of dirt, rock, and sand have been moving downstream at an alarming rate.

If the sediment gets too close to the dam's turbines, Dohrenwend says, it could ruin them completely. "The turbines rotate extremely rapidly," he says. "It would take very little sediment to destroy the turbines. With any abrasive material, it wouldn't take any time at all."

In any case, the water level could soon be so low that it won't even flow through the dam anymore. This would cut off the electricity supply altogether. Downstream, the Grand Canyon could dry up.

IMPACT

As scientists continue to study what causes droughts and what kind of impact they can have, it'll be essential for governments and citizens to change their behavior, Dohrenwend says.

If people want to continue living with cheap electricity and clean water, they'll need to find ways to use less of the precious liquid. In fact, the drought in the West might just be a wakeup call for all of us, no matter where we live.

"In some ways, the problem sounds like a simple one of not enough water," Dohrenwend says. But it's really more complicated than that.

"When you start to look at what goes on in a river flowing from the mountains to the sea, all the things we as human beings use it for, and all of what actually happens during a drought, a lot of what is going to happen isn't necessarily obvious," he says. "It could cause things we don't want to happen to happen much sooner than we might think."

After Reading:

- Why could a drought affect the availability of electricity?

- How do droughts affect the quality of drinking water?

- In the article, Emily Sohn suggests that the drought cycle in the Southwest "feeds on itself." What does she mean? Who are the most important contributors to such a cycle?

- If you were the governor of a state or the mayor of a large city in an area affected by a severe drought, what measures would you take to conserve water and maintain water supplies?

Section 2

Natural
Disasters

No one is completely safe from the threat of natural disasters. If you live near a coastline, you face the danger of hurricanes with violent winds and rain. If you live on flat lands, you are exposed to the possibility of tornadoes that can rip trees right out of the ground and even tear entire houses off their foundations. And, depending on what the Earth is like beneath you, you may face the threat of an earthquake that can make the ground tremble and cause horrific damage to even the sturdiest buildings. Luckily, all of these terrible natural disasters are relatively rare—but they do happen.

In December 2004, one of the worst natural disasters in history killed more than 150,000 people over a wide range of Asia after an earthquake triggered a massive tsunami in the Indian Ocean that washed away whole villages and completely destroyed all traces of civilized life (opposite). In our own corner of the world, Hurricane Katrina ravaged the Gulf Coast and left parts of Louisiana, Mississippi, and Alabama in ruins.

What causes these terrible events? Is there any way to prevent them? If they cannot be prevented, might there be some way to find out that they are about to happen before they wreak havoc and claim lives? In the following section, we examine some of the world's most dangerous natural phenomena and the important work scientists are doing to try to make the world safer in the face of these sometimes unpredictable events. From the raging waters of a tsunami to the molten lava flow of a volcano, this section explores natural disasters in all their awful glory and power.

—The Editor

Tsunamis Take a Terrible Toll

The tsunami disaster of December 26, 2004, shocked the world. Besides the unthinkable cost in terms of human life—more than 150,000 people were killed—the gigantic wave from the Indian Ocean completely washed away entire towns, leaving nothing but rubble in its wake. What exactly is a tsunami? Is there any way to prevent one from happening, or at least from destroying so many lives? In the following two articles, writer Emily Sohn explores the terrible power of tsunamis and the science of predicting them.

—The Editor

Wave of Destruction

by Emily Sohn

Before Reading:

- What are some of the natural dangers that people living near the ocean could face?

- Why do many people live close to the water?

- Could there be a tsunami where you live? Why or why not?

It was a nightmare come true.

On December 26, 2004, a huge wall of water rose from the Indian Ocean and slammed into the coasts of countries in Asia and Africa. The giant wave, called a **tsunami**, washed people out of their homes and swept them off beaches.

From Indonesia and Thailand to India and Somalia, the terrifying wave left more than 150,000 people dead. Millions lost their homes. It was one of the most deadly and destructive natural disasters in recent history.

Volunteer organizations and governments around the world rushed to help. Meanwhile, many scientists are looking at the disaster as a major wakeup call. Systems for detecting tsunamis and warning people that one is coming just aren't good enough in many places, critics say.

Scientists are now trying to find ways to do a better job of detecting tsunamis and providing timely warnings of danger.

RARE EVENTS

Tsunamis are a natural product of Earth's **geology**. They're caused by underwater earthquakes, volcanic eruptions, or landslides. There's no way to stop them from forming. And there's no way to know exactly when or where one will hit next.

• **What causes a tsunami?**

Tsunamis are also extremely rare. So, there's not a lot of data to work with.

Instead, tsunami researchers rely on computers to try to figure out where waves might start and how they might behave. Some projects focus on predicting tsunamis. Others look at how such waves move and what happens when they hit land.

In a few places, such as Oregon State University in Corvallis, researchers even use wave machines that produce mini-tsunamis in the laboratory.

"We're pretty good at knowing where [a tsunami] is going to go and how long it would take to get there," says Robert Dalrymple. He's a coastal engineer at Johns

Hopkins University in Baltimore.

"What I think is the hard part," he says, "is figuring out what happens when the wave gets to shore. How does it go around **breakwaters**? How does it break? How does it run up on land and around structures?"

- **What may be the hardest part in predicting tsunamis?**

TSUNAMI BASICS

Tsunami is a Japanese word meaning "harbor wave." Most tsunamis form after a massive underwater earthquake. The 2004 Indian Ocean tsunami, for instance, was triggered by a powerful quake at the bottom of the ocean near the west coast of an island in Indonesia called Sumatra.

The Indian Ocean quake happened at a place called a **fault line**, where one of Earth's giant **plates** slipped underneath another. This pushed the top plate up as much as 15 feet [4.6 meters] over 600 miles [966 km] of its length. The result was a ripple of major waves in all directions.

The types of waves that you usually see at the beach are actually formed by an up-and-down motion of the water. Tsunamis, instead, push massive amounts of water in one direction. They can move as fast as 500 miles [805 km] per hour.

- **Where did the 2004 Indian Ocean quake take place?**

As scary as the gargantuan waves sound, tsunamis are rare enough that you shouldn't let worry about them affect your life. "The probability of having an earthquake and a tsunami when you go to the beach is pretty slim," Dalrymple says. "I would still go to the beach."

Still, knowing where tsunamis might happen and what signs to look for can be useful. One area of concern is a fault line in Monterey Bay, California. Another is a volcano in the Canary Islands off the northwest coast of Africa. Should the volcano erupt, it could set off a tsunami that would flood New York.

HIGH RISKS

By far the highest risk is in the Pacific Ocean, especially near Japan and Hawaii. That's where most tsunami monitoring happens.

Scientists are keeping a close eye on a Pacific fault called Cascadia. A major tsunami struck there in 1700. Elsewhere in the Pacific, tsunamis caused by a massive underwater landslide off Papua New Guinea killed 2,100 people in 1998.

Scattered throughout the Pacific region, six special detectors sit and wait for changes in water pressure, which would signal a tsunami. When the detectors sense a change, they send signals to a buoy on the surface, which then transmits signals to a satellite in space.

Within minutes, the message arrives at centers in Hawaii and Alaska. Sirens follow to warn people to move inland.

There's no such system in the Indian Ocean. That's one big reason why the December 2004 tsunami was so catastrophic. Very few people knew that a giant wave was on its way.

Even when monitoring is in place, you still need ways to warn large numbers of people very quickly about an impending disaster.

PUBLIC EDUCATION

Public education programs could help prevent future deaths, Dalrymple says.

As a tsunami approaches, beaches can actually get wider as water recedes before the waves arrive. In

> • **Describe the warning signs that indicate a tsunami might strike.**

places such as Thailand, people went exploring on the newly exposed sand, only to be struck by huge waves that can move as fast as 30 miles [48 km] per hour when they hit land. You can't outrun a tsunami.

It's also important to know that tsunamis often arrive in several waves up to 90 minutes apart. The first wave isn't always the biggest. So, if one major wave hits, get to a safe spot and stay there for longer than you might otherwise think is necessary.

The location and construction of buildings can make a difference, too.

To predict what kind of damage a tsunami might cause depending on the lay of the land, Dalrymple uses mathematics to describe the motion of water. Then, he includes factors that change the way a wave breaks, such as the shape of the coastline, the width and steepness of beaches, the size of reefs, and canals and rivers that allow water to rush inland.

"You start out by doing lots of idealized waves," Dalrymple says. "Then you look at possible shapes, waves on different slopes, waves running around walls of buildings. Then you create a catalog of all the different situations."

Dalrymple is interested in figuring out how to design buildings in tsunami zones to reduce damage. Although his research is still at an early stage, he already has some recommendations for tsunami defense.

Houses on stilts are one possibility. Another is to build protective walls that block out the sea. People in Japan sometimes do that already.

- **How might Dalrymple's use of mathematics help reduce tsunami damage?**

AFTERMATH

There are dangers even after a tsunami hits. One fear is that diseases such as cholera will spread if people can't get access to clean drinking water. Malaria and dengue fever are also concerns in the affected areas around the Indian Ocean.

"Water rushing in from the Indian Ocean can create pools of water where they didn't exist before," says Crispin Pierce. He's a professor of environmental public health at the University of Wisconsin, Eau Claire.

In some places, water flooded coastal areas as far as 1 kilometer [0.62 miles] inland, Pierce says.

Saltwater and polluted runoff can get into drinking water, making people sick. Disease-carrying mosquitoes also have more places to breed when there's a lot of water around.

So far, Pierce says, there hasn't been a big surge in disease. That's one positive note amid lots of sad news.

As long as people continue donating money for food, water, and medical care, and there are ways to get supplies to affected populations, the tragedy might not grow any worse. Pierce encourages kids to donate their allowances to relief organizations if they want to do something to help.

In the meantime, analysis and research continues. You can't stop

- **Besides the destruction caused by a tsunami, what other effects could such a disaster cause? Name at least three that could create great concern among people.**

the earth from cracking and groaning at unpredictable times. You can, however, prepare yourself to react in the best possible way, not only to giant waves but also to other natural disasters that might come your way.

After Reading:

- When scientists detect that a tsunami is coming, what do you think would be the best way to warn people? What do you think would make a good warning system?

- How would a warning system for tsunamis be different from a warning system for hurricanes or tornadoes?

- Come up with an idea for raising money for tsunami victims.

- What sorts of researchers would study tsunamis? Come up with at least two different types of scientists or engineers who might be interested in the phenomenon.

- Design and draw a picture of a house that you think would be safe in a tsunami. Be sure to label all the parts. Given that many of the people whose homes were destroyed have little money, how might you make this house affordable for these people?

- Why is it difficult to predict where a tsunami wave will break?

Digging Into a Tsunami Disaster

by Emily Sohn

The date December 26, 2004, will be long remembered by many people. First, there was a powerful earthquake at the bottom of the Indian Ocean. Then, a massive wave called a tsunami spread out in all directions. When the wave hit the shores of nations surrounding the ocean, more than 145,000 people died.

Now, scientists are using computers and other tools to study how this catastrophic event changed Earth.

The Indian Ocean earthquake was the largest one in 40 years. On the Richter scale, which rates the strength of earthquakes, the event scored 9.0. That's about as strong as earthquakes get.

The quake occurred just north of an island in Indonesia called Simeulue. This spot is located in a zone where two immense sections of Earth's surface—called plates—meet. One section, called the India plate, is slowly sliding under the other section, called the Burma plate, at a rate of about 6 centimeters [2.4 in] per year.

In the 2004 quake, the sudden slippage was much larger. In some places, the plates may have been shoved as much as 20 meters (66 feet) past each other. And some slippage occurred all along 1,200 kilometers [746 miles] of the boundary between the plates. That's longer than the state of California!

Where the shifting was most extreme, parts of the seafloor suddenly jerked up as much as 5 meters (16 feet). All of the water above the uplifted ground had to move as a result. That's what caused the tsunami.

Computer studies by Chen Ji, a **seismologist** at the California Institute of Technology in Pasadena, show that waves raced away from the quake site as fast as a jetliner. The first crash of water hit Sumatra 15 minutes after the quake, with waves as high as 15 meters (49 feet).

Tsunamis hit Thailand 75 minutes after the earthquake. They hit Sri Lanka and India 4 hours after it happened. Disaster even reached as far as Africa. People died in Somalia and Kenya, some 5,000 kilometers (3,100 miles) away from the quake's center.

Earth is different now. Besides all the wreckage that needs to be cleaned up and the sadness that must be dealt with, some parts of the ocean floor are higher than they were. Some areas are lower.

There have also been changes in Earth's spin. When the India plate moved closer toward Earth's center, the planet became like a spinning figure skater who pulls her arms closer to her body. Earth started spinning more quickly. Its daily rotation is now about 2.67 milliseconds faster than it was before.

Earth can feel so solid when you're standing on it. It's amazing how quickly everything can get shaken up.

Going Deeper:

Perkins, Sid. "Tsunami Disaster: Scientists Model the Big Quake and Its Consequences." *Science News* 167 (January 8, 2005): 19. Available online at *http://www.sciencenews.org/articles/ 20050108/fob1.asp*.

Additional information about the Indian Ocean tsunami of December 26, 2004, can be found online at *www.pmel.noaa.gov/tsunami/ sumatra20041226.html* and *www.ngdc.noaa.gov/ spotlight/tsunami/tsunami.html*.

Predicting Earthquakes

How many lives would be saved each year if scientists could pinpoint when and where an earthquake was about to happen and alert people so they could take shelter and protect their most valuable possessions? This question has long been pondered by earth scientists, and, as writer Emily Sohn demonstrates in the next article, the answer may be just over the horizon.

—The Editor

Quick Quake Alerts

by Emily Sohn

The ground shakes. Dishes fall off shelves. Houses collapse. Cars topple over bridges. Every year, earthquakes destroy homes and schools, and they kill many thousands of people around the world (Figure 2.1). Even scarier, it's impossible to know exactly when and where the next one will strike.

A system of detectors in Los Angeles might be able to warn that an earthquake is coming, according to a new analysis. Even if the alarm comes only a few seconds before the quake, the system could save lives.

Earthquakes cause a few different kinds of underground vibrations. One kind are called **P waves**, which travel quickly through Earth and rarely cause damage. The **S waves** that follow are more dangerous. They travel half as fast and shake the ground from side to side.

Richard M. Allen of the University of Wisconsin-Madison and his colleagues analyzed ground motions from 53 fairly strong earthquakes that have struck Los Angeles since 1995 (Figure 2.2). By looking at the first few seconds of a quake's P wave, they found they could predict how big the oncoming S wave would be.

Using detectors already in place throughout Los

Figure 2.1 **This photograph of a severely damaged medical building was taken after a serious earthquake hit Los Angeles in 1994.**

The Richter Scale

Descriptor	Magnitude	Effects	Frequency of Occurrence
Micro	Less than 2.0	Microearthquakes, not felt	8,000 per day
Very minor	2.0–2.9	Generally not felt, but recorded	About 1,000 per day
Minor	3.0–3.9	Often felt, but rarely causes damage	About 49,000 per year
Light	4.0–4.9	Noticeable shaking of indoor items, rattling noises; significant damage unlikely	About 6,200 per year
Moderate	5.0–5.9	Can cause major damage to poorly constructed buildings over small regions. At most slight damage to well-designed buildings	800 per year
Strong	6.0–6.9	Can be destructive in areas up to about 100 miles [161 km] across in populated areas	120 per year
Major	7.0–7.9	Can cause serious damage over larger areas	18 per year
Great	8.0–8.9	Can cause serious damage in areas several hundred miles across	1 per year
Rare Great	9.0 or greater	Devastating in areas several thousand miles across	1 per 20 years

Figure 2.2 The Richter scale helps earth scientists pinpoint the strength, or magnitude, of earthquakes.

Angeles could give residents at least a few seconds warning that a quake is coming, Allen suggests. That wouldn't be enough time to run away. But a siren or Internet message could save lives by giving people time to shut off power and stop trains. Kids in school could dive under their desks.

The system wouldn't make earthquakes any less scary, but at least you'd know what was coming!

Going Deeper:

Perkins, Sid. "Sensing a Vibe: Seismic-alert System Could Give Los Angeles a Few Seconds' Warning." *Science News* **163 (May 3, 2003): 276. Available online at** *http://www.sciencenews.org/20030503/ fob3.asp*.

Effects of Earthquakes

Earthquakes may do a lot of obvious damage—laying waste to highways and bridges and causing skyscrapers to collapse into piles of jagged rubble. But they also have powerful, yet subtle, influences. Even a distant earthquake can profoundly affect the way the water deep below the Earth's surface behaves. As writer Emily Sohn explains in the following article, scientists have noted some bizarre earthquake-related changes in the way geysers erupt.

—The Editor

Distant Quake Changes Geyser Eruptions

by Emily Sohn

Underground, Yellowstone National Park in Wyoming is an exciting place. With more than 10,000 geysers, hot springs, and steaming volcanic vents, there's always something spewing, spouting, or bubbling over.

Scientists recently turned up a new surprise at Yellowstone. Amazingly, an earthquake that shook Alaska on November 3, 2002, affected underground activity in Yellowstone more than 3,100 kilometers [1,926 miles] away, say geologists from the University of Utah in Salt Lake City.

The earthquake had an especially large effect on some of the geysers in the park (Figure 2.3). Geysers are spouts of water that shoot out of the ground at periodic intervals. The park uses instruments to monitor 22 geysers around the clock. Of those, eight changed their patterns for a few weeks after the quake, records show.

Some geysers, such as Daisy Geyser, erupted more often for a few weeks after the quake. Others, such as Lone Pine Geyser, erupted less often. The researchers think underground vibrations traveling all the way from Alaska loosened mineral deposits that normally regulate

Figure 2.3 Earthquakes as far away as Alaska can affect how often geysers like this one in Yellowstone National Park erupt.

geyser eruptions. The famous geyser Old Faithful wasn't affected at all.

The quake influenced some of the park's hot springs, too. A few springs that are normally calm surged into a raging boil. A spring that's normally clear turned muddy.

That's a long, long way over which an earthquake's effects can be felt!

Going Deeper:

Perkins, Sid. "Geyser Bashing: Distant Quake Alters Timing of Eruptions." *Science News* 165 (June 5, 2004): 357. Available online at *http://www.sciencenews.org/articles/20040605/fob5.asp*.

Volcanoes and Earthquakes: Related Disasters

You probably have a pretty clear mental image of what an erupting volcano looks like. Hot ash and smoke burst from the volcano's crater, and red-hot lava streams down the hillside. You might also be able to imagine an earthquake: The ground shakes violently, objects fall from shelves, and the Earth may crack underfoot. What if earthquakes could help predict when a volcano is about to erupt? As writer Kate Ramsayer shows in the following article, scientists have recently found that these two powerful types of natural disasters may, in fact, be related.

—The Editor

A Volcano Wakes Up

by Kate Ramsayer

Before Reading:

- **How are earthquakes and volcanoes related?**

- **Why can volcanoes be found in some areas of the world but not in others?**

After resting for nearly two decades, Mount St. Helens woke up in the fall of 2004. Shaking ground and a skyward blast proved to the world that it's still an active volcano.

Tiny earthquakes had been shaking the mountain for a week before it erupted on October 1, 2004. The volcano spewed a gray plume of steam and ash 10,000 feet [3,048 meters] into the air. Hot **magma** began oozing out of the crater a few weeks later. As it kept coming, the magma literally built a small mountain in front of scientists' eyes.

These events weren't as explosive as the massive eruption that blew the top off the mountain in 1980. But the recent activity at Mount St. Helens has kept scientists busy making observations and trying to guess what comes next.

"All of us geologists are curious to see what's going to happen," says Tom Pierson. He's a research geologist with the U.S. Geological Survey.

If you thought that a volcano near your house was about to erupt, what would you do? If you're like me and hundreds of other residents of the Pacific Northwest, you'd pack a picnic lunch and try to find the best viewing spot!

On October 2, 2004, the day after Mount St. Helens belched a little steam and ash for the first time in a long while, I drove out to the Johnston Ridge Observatory at the Mount St. Helens National Volcanic Monument. It's the closest visitor's center to the volcano. Scientists were saying that it was very possible that the volcano would erupt again, so I was hoping to have a front row seat.

I was definitely not the only one with that idea. The parking lot, which holds more than 350 cars, was almost full. People were lining up along the rails of the overlook, cameras set up on tripods, pointed at the mountain, so that they would be ready if the volcano blew. The visitor's center was packed with people looking at models of the volcano and watching the needle on the seismograph, which measures earth movement, jerk up and down with the swarms of tiny earthquakes in the crater.

Unfortunately, I got to the observatory about one hour after a steam burst had escaped from the mountain, but I was determined to catch the next bit of excitement. As I waited, I talked with one of the park rangers. He said that scientists studying the volcano were about to give a press conference at another lookout down the road. So I hopped back in my car and joined TV news crews and newspaper reporters from around the country to hear the latest updates.

I was at the media gathering place for only half an hour when we noticed a long stream of cars going back down the mountain. The U.S. Forest Service had closed the observatory because rangers thought that an eruption could happen at any moment. So everyone had to retreat to another visitor's center farther away from Mount St. Helens.

The only thing that would have made it more exciting would have been if the volcano had actually erupted! Unfortunately for me, even though I waited until it got dark that Saturday and then came back on Sunday, the only movement I saw on the volcano was some rockslides.

Still, it was a beautiful fall weekend, and I got to spend it outside, meeting people and talking with other reporters, sharing guesses about when, or if, the volcano would erupt. We were all afraid to leave, because we were sure that something would happen just as soon as we got out of sight.

"Everybody's really excited and wants to see anything, but unfortunately I can't push the button," says Alison Eckberg. She's a park ranger at the Coldwater Ridge Visitors Center, which filled up when the Johnston Ridge Observatory was closed.

"I'd like to see it explode, to see some kind of action. That would be amazing," 15-year-old Nicki Tarr says. She lives in Tigard, Oregon, and had come to watch the volcano with her family. The Tarrs had good seats at an overlook, but hundreds of other people simply parked along the road and pointed their folding chairs towards the mountain.

Families and friends brought Frisbees®, footballs, books, and barbecues to pass the time. Although there was only that little steam burst on Saturday morning, nobody I talked to wished that they had stayed home that weekend.

"You couldn't ask for a better day to stand and watch a volcano," says Paul McKerracher, who was at the Coldwater Ridge Observatory.

I agreed.

MAKING A VOLCANO

Mount St. Helens is in Washington State. It's part of the Cascade Mountain Range, which stretches from British Columbia in Canada to northern California.

Mountains in the Cascades formed where two big chunks of Earth's crust, called plates, ran into each other. When the plate under the Pacific Ocean pushed beneath the plate under North America, the incredibly high pressure and temperature caused rocks to melt into a gooey, superheated magma. The magma then seeped up through the crust. Occasionally, it reached the surface, creating volcanoes.

On the morning of May 18, 1980, Mount St. Helens demonstrated this ongoing process. The mountain erupted, sending ash more than 15 miles [24 km] into the sky (Figure 2.4). The blast also went outwards, blowing out the north face of the mountain. This outburst caused massive landslides and leveled trees for miles. Lasting for 9 hours, the eruption killed 57 people.

Over the next 6 years, there were some small eruptions. At times, magma seeped out of the crater, creating a lava dome. Then, except for a few minor outbursts, all was pretty quiet on Mount St. Helens for about 18 years.

• **What happened at Mount St. Helens on May 18, 1980?**

Figure 2.4 Mount St. Helens erupted on May 18, 1980. Then, in the fall of 2004, it became active again. This photograph was taken during the May 1980 eruption.

PUZZLING EARTHQUAKES

When a swarm of small earthquakes started up in late September 2004, it puzzled geologists. On Mount St. Helens, earthquakes usually mean that fresh magma filled with expanding gases is pushing toward the surface, shoving rocks aside.

Scientists can detect these gases, including sulfur dioxide and carbon dioxide, using a special airplane that collects air samples. But when they made flights in the early fall of 2004, the air didn't have unusual amounts of the gases.

- **What gases are scientists looking for when they fly over Mount St. Helens?**

This would normally suggest that old magma was triggering the earthquakes. Like a flat soda, this magma would have already lost its gas, and the volcano probably wouldn't erupt explosively.

But the earthquakes became more frequent and stronger as time went on. Altogether, they released more energy than had been released since the 1980 eruption. This didn't fit with the old-magma hypothesis, Pierson says.

So geologists came up with a new hypothesis. Maybe fresh magma was causing the ruckus on Mount St. Helens. But airplanes couldn't detect any released gas because it was being absorbed by the crater's glacier.

Then seismographs, which record ground movements, detected something called a **harmonic tremor**. A harmonic tremor is a slow vibration of the ground. It's a bit like the rattling sound you sometimes hear when water flows through pipes, Pierson says.

This ground motion told scientists that fresh magma was definitely on the move.

"Each one of these tremor events means the magma moved a little further," says Jim Vallance. He's a research geologist with the Cascades Volcano Observatory and the U.S. Geological Survey.

The increasing tremors and moving magma indicated that an eruption could occur within 24 hours of the first blast. On October 2, 2004, scientists and park rangers with the U.S. Forest Service decided to move hundreds of volcano watchers back for safety.

> • **Describe a harmonic tremor.**

"When you see a really strong tremor, it's a good time to give the volcano a little room," Bill Steele says. He's the seismic laboratory coordinator at the Pacific Northwest Seismograph Network at the University of Washington.

However, nothing happened that weekend, showing that nobody can predict exactly what a volcano might do. Since then, the mountain has released several, small plumes of steam and ash.

A NEW DOME

Many scientists are now excited about the creation of a new **lava dome** in the **crater** of Mount St. Helens. Since mid-October 2004, magma has been breaking through the surface at a rate of about 7 or 8 cubic yards [5 or 6 cubic meters] per second.

"That's like having a dump truck or cement mixer full of magma ejected every second onto the dome," Steele says. "It's pretty phenomenal." Scientists can practically watch a mountain being built right before their eyes.

Warning! Warning!

Many popular science-fiction movies and novels look at how a natural disaster, such as a volcano eruption, might affect us. A common plot device is to have a lone scientist trying to warn those around him or her, only to be ignored. Another is to have people in the area unprepared for the disaster until it strikes. The combination leads to panic and confusion. This makes an exciting and dramatic story. In real life, however, no one wants panic or confusion to occur. Lives could be lost.

In real life, groups of scientists and other observers work together to predict natural events and provide warnings of potential threats, from major storms and heat waves to earthquakes and volcanoes. For examples of such predictions and warnings, see *www.disastercenter.com/*.

People can prepare for such possible disasters as well. What can they do?

Challenge: An Evacuation Plan

Imagine you live near a volcano, such as Mount St. Helens. The volcano has been quiet for many years, but scientists are warning that an explosive eruption may occur soon. They ask local residents to create an evacuation plan for their families. Make one for your family. Think about the following aspects.

1. How will you stay aware of the situation? Hint: How will you continue to receive information, even in a power failure?
2. What should you have in your home? Hint: What if you are ordered to stay indoors for several days because of falling ash?
3. What should you have ready to take if you have to leave? Hint: What can you easily carry?
4. How would you prepare your home for the time that you would be away? Hint: What might threaten your home while you are gone? Power failures? Water damage?
5. If told to evacuate, where will you go and how will you get there? Hint: Where would you look for information on how best to leave your area?

You can find helpful information on evacuation plans at *www.disastercenter.com/guide/landslide.html*.

Show your plan to others and ask for input. Make any changes to improve your plan. When you are satisfied, turn your evacuation plan into a poster or Web page for your family or friends.

Will the dome continue to grow, or will the volcano take another rest? That's the big question, says Willie Scott of the U.S. Geological Survey. There's no reliable way for geologists to predict what a volcano will do.

"All we can do is monitor it closely and see if indeed it's dying down or if it's changing its behavior," Scott says. "There's no cookbook that tells us that, if we see this, this will happen."

Scientists have several ways to keep an eye on the volcano. They can measure the gases that the volcano releases. These measurements give them clues about the magma beneath the surface.

They can use seismographs to track earthquakes, which have quieted down since the magma forged a path to the surface. Although the first eruption in the fall of 2004 destroyed some instruments, others have been slung into place on the crater by helicopter to measure the shaking.

Geologists can also look for changes in the shape and size of the mountain. They can look for hotspots on the crater by detecting the heat given off by the surface. They can collect rocks to study the magma itself.

- **What might happen if the new lava dome in the crater of Mount St. Helens collapses?**

QUICK TRIPS

Most of the monitoring equipment is placed in the crater by helicopter. A few times, however, scientists have made very quick trips to the crater floor to take samples or set up instruments. They don't linger, though, because they don't want to be there if the volcano erupts!

Still, scientists want to be able to detect any changes in the mountain that could signal danger. The new dome is unstable. If it collapses and clogs the magma flow, the pressure could build up and lead to an eruption. Ash in the air could cause problems for nearby airplanes. Mudslides or floodwaters from a melted glacier could harm people near the mountain.

"Any volcano surprises the people who are studying it," Pierson says. It pays to pay attention.

After Reading:

- **What would be some of the responsibilities of geologists studying volcanoes? What would they look for? What equipment would be helpful?**

- **If Mount St. Helens erupted again as it did in 1980, how might the surrounding area be affected? In what ways might countries around the world feel the effects of such an eruption?**

- **Besides volcanoes, what other natural occurrences might cause mountains to form or disappear?**

- **In what ways might a volcanic eruption affect the environment?**

Section 3

Inside the Earth's Crust

For centuries, people have wondered what lies beneath the Earth's crust. Miners have penetrated the Earth looking for treasure in the form of gems and oil to fuel industry, while scientists have dug deep in search of answers to the lingering mysteries of how the Earth was formed. In this section, we take a trip below the surface of the Earth to explore what lies there and how it affects our daily lives.

The first article looks at the problem of reaching the center of the Earth. Although scientists have a fairly extensive conception of how the planet is constructed, no one has ever successfully probed Earth's innermost depths. Author Emily Sohn explains why a journey to the center of the Earth is so difficult and describes new techniques that might finally allow us to get there.

In today's global economy, as the oil we use to power our cars and factories becomes scarce, scientists are always searching for new kinds of fuel. As we drill deep into the Earth for gas and oil, we can learn a lot about our planet, as Emily Sohn shows in the second article.

Everyone knows that precious jewels lie deep inside the Earth. In the final article of this section, Emily Sohn describes the way emeralds are formed, and how scientists have learned new ways to determine precisely which mine of all the sites in the world a particular emerald comes from.

—The Editor

Journey to the Center of the Earth

French writer Jules Verne wrote his famous novel *Journey to the Center of the Earth* in 1864. In it, a group of adventurers makes a daring trip deep inside the Earth's crust. Since Verne's novel was published—and even for centuries before—people have wondered what lies below the Earth's surface and tried to determine how they might get there. So far, the center of the Earth has proven impossible to reach, mainly because of the difficulty of finding a force strong enough to safely blast through the many layers of solid rock and metallic elements that make up the planet. One California scientist has recently come up with an idea for a method that might be used to finally send a probe all the way into the Earth's center. In the following article, author Emily Sohn describes his findings.

—The Editor

Riding to Earth's Core

by Emily Sohn

Ever wonder what you'd find if you could travel to the center of the earth? Someday, we might find out, says geophysicist David Stevenson of the California Institute of Technology.

Stevenson has thought up a way to send a probe to Earth's core. For now, his plan is mostly just a cool idea. Quite a few obstacles keep it from being practical.

So far, the deepest anyone has drilled into the earth is 10 kilometers [6 miles]. The hard crust of continents probably goes down at least another 200 kilometers [124 miles]. Below that lies a gooey layer called the **mantle**, which surrounds a liquid outer core and a solid inner core. Both inner layers are made mostly of iron.

Stevenson's idea is to blast a hole 300 meters [984 feet] deep and 10 centimeters [4 inches] wide. Into the hole, he would pour melted iron, which would flow downward and create enough pressure to push the crack to Earth's center. He estimates it would take the probe about a week to get there.

Blasting a big enough crack would take about the same amount of energy as that contained in a basic hydrogen bomb.

Journey to Earth's Center by Ivars Peterson

The idea that Earth might be hollow, with winding underground passages and vast underworlds of fantastic creatures, has been around for a long time. Such an Earth has been the setting for a variety of thrilling stories, movies, and TV shows.

One of the earliest examples is the science-fiction novel *Journey to the Center of the Earth* by French writer Jules Verne. He wrote it in 1864.

In the story, a group of adventurers travel to Iceland and descend into the crater of an extinct volcano. The explorers encounter various hazards as they trek deep into Earth. They end up at a vast underground sea, where they stumble upon prehistoric animals and a forest of 40-foot-tall mushrooms. Building a raft, they cross the ocean, battling gigantic sea monsters along the way. After further adventures, the explorers hurtle back to Earth's surface atop a river of lava. They eventually find themselves on a mountainside on the island of Stromboli in Italy.

Verne's heroes actually didn't get very far toward Earth's center. And if they had, they would have faced intense heat, immense pressure, and an iron core. Even without these factors, gravity would have been an issue.

When you drop a stone, it falls to the ground, pulled by Earth's **gravity**. In fact, there's a gravitational attraction between any two bodies. The strength of this force depends on the mass of each of the two bodies and how far apart they are. A larger mass means a larger force, so the sun has a much larger gravitational attraction than does Earth or an apple. Also, the farther apart two objects are, the less force they exert on each other.

Earth's gravitational force keeps the moon in orbit around Earth, governs the arcing path of a baseball, ensures that a dropped apple hits the ground, and keeps you from floating away.

At Earth's surface, you're attracted by all of Earth. As you travel toward Earth's center, you're attracted by parts of Earth that are both above and below you. So, the force pulling on you gets smaller as you get closer to the center of Earth. At the center itself, you would be weightless. You're attracted equally in all directions, so there would be no net gravitational force acting on you. Everything cancels out.

It would be interesting to imagine what Verne's heroes might have done if they had made it all the way to Earth's center and encountered weightlessness.

The biggest challenge would be building the probe. The center of the earth gets so hot and there is so much pressure that most metals would melt. Electronic equipment would fall apart.

If scientists can ever find a way around those obstacles, they might get a new view of some of Earth's deepest secrets.

Going Deeper:

Perkins, Sid. "Going Down? Probe to Ride to Earth's Core in a Mass of Molten Iron." *Science News* **163 (May 17, 2003): 307–308. Available online at** *http://www.sciencenews.org/ 20030517/fob2.asp*.

Finding Fuels

In recent months, gas prices have soared to record heights, leading people to wonder if there is any other type of fuel that might replace our need for huge supplies of oil to run our cars and power our factories. Scientists are always on the lookout for new sources of fuel, from natural gas to pockets of oil. As they search the inside of the Earth, they learn more not only about fuel, but also about the makeup of the planet and the possibility of unknown life-forms existing in places that have never yet been explored.

—The Editor

Drilling Deep for Fuel

by Emily Sohn

Digging in dirt and rock is a big business. Oil and gas lie beneath Earth's surface in certain places, and these reservoirs are the planet's main sources of fuel.

Until now, all the digging has happened only in Earth's outer layer, called the crust. Oil and gas wells normally go no deeper than about 6 kilometers [4 miles]. A new study shows that natural gas, mainly methane, may also form in a much deeper layer called the mantle. This means that new sources of energy could lie at depths of 100 kilometers (62 miles) or more.

Oil and gas found near Earth's surface are often described as **fossil fuels**. Most scientists favor the idea that these hydrocarbon fuels were formed by the breakdown of ancient plants and animals. However, recent research also shows that methane gas can form in the crust when there are no living creatures around.

Researchers from Indiana University, South Bend wondered if this could also happen deeper down. So they did a lab experiment to simulate conditions in the mantle. They combined materials normally found at those depths. Then they put the mixture under extreme heat and pressure.

The experiment produced tiny bubbles of methane gas, the scientists report. However, no one knows yet how much methane, if any, is actually present in the mantle, and, if it is present, whether any gas might seep up into the crust and emerge from spots on the ocean floor.

The research could provide important clues about how life began on Earth. Some bacteria feed on methane. If methane were present in the mantle, it could support populations of **microbes**, allowing them to survive in such an extreme environment. It may also be worth looking for underground stores of methane on Mars and other planets when searching for signs of life.

Going Deeper:

Goho, Alexandra. "Deep Squeeze: Experiments Point to Methane in Earth's Mantle." *Science News* 166 (September 25, 2004): 198. Available online at *http://www.sciencenews.org/articles/20040925/fob7.asp*.

Information about the origin of fossil fuels can be found online at *http://www.all-science-fair-projects.com/science_fair_projects_encyclopedia/Fossil_fuel*.

Identifying Emeralds

Emeralds are among the rarest and most valuable stones on Earth. The deep green gems, which are mined all over the world, are set into jewelry and sold for huge profits. But up until recently, it was impossible to tell the site from which a given emerald came just by looking at it. As Emily Sohn shows in the next article, scientists may have found a way to use the unique molecular makeup of different emeralds to pinpoint their source—and their value.

—The Editor

Unscrambling a Gem of a Mystery

by Emily Sohn

Hidden inside every shiny green emerald is a geographical mystery.

Once an emerald is plucked from a mine in its home country and turned into a piece of jewelry, it can be nearly impossible to figure out where the gem came from in the first place. Now, researchers from France think they have found a solution.

It's all about the water. Molecules of water are trapped inside tiny channels in every emerald (Figure 3.1). Water has the chemical formula H_2O. This means that each molecule of water is made up of three atoms: two atoms of hydrogen (H) and one atom of oxygen (O).

There are several types of hydrogen atoms. One unusual type, called **deuterium**, weighs twice as much as the type of hydrogen most commonly found. Some water molecules contain the heavier form of hydrogen instead of the lighter one.

It turns out that when you shine a special kind of laser light on an emerald, the heavy hydrogen reacts differently in emeralds from different parts of the world. This signal reveals where a certain emerald came from.

So far, the researchers have used their method to trace

Figure 3.1 Emeralds are some of the world's most valuable gems. They can be seen here in their natural form, before being carefully cleared and set into jewelry.

emeralds to 10 specific mines in seven countries. They can also tell the difference between natural emeralds and human-made ones.

Emeralds from some countries cost more than others, so the new technique might help jewelry sellers determine how much their gems are truly worth. It could also help historians trace ancient trade routes.

So, every gem carries its own story, and researchers are starting to translate it into a language that we can all understand.

Going Deeper:

Goho, Alexandra. "Gemstone Geography: New Technique Discerns Emeralds' Beginnings." *Science News* 164 (December 13, 2003): 371. Available online at *http://www.sciencenews.org/20031213/fob1.asp*.

Section 4

Under the Sea

The vast majority of our planet is covered in water, but much of what lies below the oceans remains a mystery, even to the scientists who study it. In recent years, people have been working harder than ever to solve the mystery and to find out just what kinds of things—both living and nonliving—exist in the darkest depths of the sea. In this section, we explore some of the findings that have been made.

In the first article, author Kate Ramsayer traces the journey of the ship *JOIDES Resolution*, which is devoted to exploring the depths of the ocean and the lifeforms that may be found there by drilling holes in the sea floor.

The second article explores the strange phenomenon of ocean avalanches. Although you probably know how much damage an avalanche in the mountains can cause, you might be surprised to learn that avalanches also happen under the sea, as author Sorcha McDonagh explains.

In the third article, writer Emily Sohn takes a look at a unique underwater formation called the Lost City. Found off the coast of Bermuda, this complex system of rock structures is home to undersea vents that have been active for tens of thousands of years.

Finally, we dive under the water with Alvin, a submersible vessel that has been exploring the undersea world for years, with some impressive success.

—The Editor

The *Resolution* Explores Under the Sea

In the following article, author Kate Ramsayer looks at the work of a special scientific ship called the *Resolution*, which is working to figure out what kinds of rock, mud, and fossils make up the crust of the Earth at the bottom of the ocean. Thanks to the ship—which acts as a sort of "floating university"—and its determined crew, scientists have been able to learn a great deal about the "plumbing system" of the Earth.

—The Editor

Deep Drilling at Sea

by Kate Ramsayer

Before Reading:

- **What sorts of things would you expect to find if you drilled into the ocean floor?**

- **Why would scientists do research aboard a ship at sea?**

Beakers and chemical bottles sit on shelves, just like in a normal science lab. High-powered microscopes, **incubators** for growing bacteria, and other equipment line the room, just like in a normal science lab.

But, once you feel the floor start to sway or you look out the windows only to see a vast expanse of blue, you know this is no typical science lab. Instead, the seven floors of research space are a "floating university" on board a ship called the *JOIDES Resolution*.

In June 2004 , the 60 scientists aboard the *Resolution* set sail for the waters off British Columbia. They drilled holes deep into the ocean floor and conducted experiments that they hope will provide clues about what's happening in these largely unexplored areas.

- **What is the *JOIDES Resolution*?**

"We know more about Mars and the moon than we do about the ocean and its evolution," says Steve Bohlen. He's president of the Joint Oceanographic Institutes, the organization that manages the expedition.

NEWS DETECTIVE by Kate Ramsayer

Before I started writing about scientific discoveries, I worked at various times in research labs. But I've never seen a place quite like the *JOIDES Resolution*.

The labs, conference rooms, sleeping quarters, offices, and lounges are arranged on seven floors. As I toured the ship with other journalists and a few land-based scientists, I found myself going up and down different staircases and weaving through windowless rooms. I often had no idea which floor I was on or in what direction I was facing. I quickly realized that, if I had to work on this mazelike vessel, it would take me a while to find my way around.

During the tour, I also started wondering if I would enjoy working in this kind of environment. All the scientists who had been on similar trips mentioned the constant noise of the drilling equipment, which might make it hard to sleep or concentrate on experiments. And while the large size of the ship makes it relatively steady in the ocean waves, it could still be a miserable 50 or more days for anyone who happened to get seasick easily. Plus, I'd miss my family and friends if I were away for such a long time.

In September 2004, the ship was in waters off Costa Rica, drilling more holes deep into the seafloor. It will later head for the North Atlantic, looking for evidence of climate change in the distant past.

Still, if I were a geologist or a microbiologist or a chemist, such an expedition would be worth the discomfort. The scientists on the journey have an amazing opportunity to study areas of Earth that have never been looked at before.

It would be exciting to examine a piece of a core that was hundreds of feet below the seafloor just minutes before and try to figure out what it tells us about Earth's past. It would also be fun to meet other scientists from around the world who are excited about investigating a wide range of questions about the rocks and critters beneath the ocean.

While the living conditions on the ship might be tough, and working 12 hours a day for almost 2 months straight might get exhausting, I think that conducting experiments on board this research vessel would be an opportunity that I couldn't pass up.

DEEP KNOWLEDGE

To study the layers of mud, silt, and rock that lie beneath the sea, scientists take core samples. They gather these long tubes of material by drilling a narrow, vertical hole into the crust. The researchers then analyze the material, layer by layer.

A tube's different layers of rocks and sand and tiny fossils of ancient organisms provide a timeline of what happened on Earth in a given location over the last 200 million years or so.

The first ocean drilling program in 1968 gave scientists evidence that Earth's crust was divided into huge plates. These plates slowly move around, spreading apart, slipping under, or rubbing past each other.

Since then, researchers have used cores from around the world to track changes in climate or understand why some areas are rattled by earthquakes. One core drilled near Florida contained greenish glassy particles. Geologists say the particles are evidence that a hefty meteorite slammed into the Gulf of Mexico 65 million years ago.

- **When did the ocean drilling program begin, and what was one of the first scientific discoveries made by researchers in the program?**

The new drilling program aims to delve even deeper into the mysteries of the ocean.

It's the biggest earth science program we have, says Andrew Fisher. He likens it to the Hubble space telescope, which astronomers have used to probe outer space and make discoveries about the universe. Fisher is a professor at the University of California, Santa Cruz, and was one of the leaders of the *Resolution*'s June 2004 expedition.

RESOLUTION RESEARCH

Research continues nonstop aboard the *Resolution*. The crew and scientists work in rotating, 12-hour shifts, with no days off, for all the days the ship is at sea. Expeditions can last as long as 55 days.

- **Explain why Andrew Fisher compares the deep sea drilling project to the Hubble space telescope.**

To gather data, an experienced crew lowers drill pipe through thousands of feet of water in order to grind through 2,000 feet [610 m] of mud and rock. Sometimes, they have to locate a hole bored into the seafloor years before so that researchers can obtain a fresh sample.

Getting the drill pipe into such a hole is like standing on top of the Empire State Building and trying to get a straw into a Coke® bottle on the ground, says staff scientist Adam Klaus of Texas A&M University in College Station.

To provide a steady platform, the ship has special engines to keep it in place, even in choppy seas.

When technicians remove a sample from the drill pipe, the call of "core on deck" brings the scientists running. They immediately label the core sample and split it down the middle. One half is carefully wrapped up and archived so that scientists can study it later.

The other half is subjected to all kinds of tests, right on the boat.

- **Describe the process that scientists go through once someone yells "core on deck."**

Microbiologists quickly isolate samples in a sterile environment so that rock-dwelling bacteria won't suffer contamination. Geologists describe the sediment layers and take measurements of their volumes, densities, and magnetic properties. Scientists box up samples to take to their home laboratories.

EARTH'S PLUMBING SYSTEM

In the holes left by the drill pipes, researchers stash sensors that detect and record temperature, pressure, and water seepage in the rock surrounding the hole. These sensors will gather data for a few years before the scientists send robot subs to collect the information.

Fisher and his colleagues plan to establish a network of sensors in the ocean floor to study water flow in Earth's crust. Eventually, they hope to be able to pump water into one hole to see if it comes out in another hole.

Such experiments will tell them more about how the "plumbing system" within Earth's rocks works.

Other investigators are excited about the tiny microbes that can live in rocks more than 2,000 feet [610 m] below the surface.

Oregon State University graduate student Mark Nielsen is interested in how the microbes store and handle energy deep within the rock. These microbes can't use **photosynthesis**—there's no sunlight—or many of the other processes used by bacteria. Nielson's samples may tell him which chemical compounds the organisms take up.

Such studies could be useful in the search for life on other planets. Some scientists have suggested that, if life exists on Jupiter's moon Europa or Saturn's moon Titan, it could resemble the microbes that dwell in the equally hostile environment of Earth's crust.

> • **What is Mark Nielsen's interest in this trip? How might his discoveries relate to other scientific work?**

LIFE ON A BOAT

Working on a research ship isn't always easy. The scientists are away from family and friends for almost two months. Although they have access to e-mail, all 110 people on board the ship must share one telephone for personal calls.

Plus, with 12-hour working days and labs that don't always have windows, a researcher's sense of time can get out of whack.

"You can't tell the day, and time doesn't matter," says Verena Heuer. She's a microbiologist from Bremen University in Germany. "It's just the sea and you and the ship," she says.

Two days before the ship's departure, Heuer and some friends took long walks. Once they were aboard, their strolling options were strictly limited.

Packing for the trip often included special personal items. Klaus brought pictures of his family. Nielsen stocked up on chocolate, Sour Patch® Kids, and books. He also bought an iPod® music player specifically for the trip. Heuer packed coffee and said that as long as she didn't run out of chocolate, she'd be a happy camper.

For the scientists, the chance to be with other scientists to share ideas, ask questions, and conduct experiments makes up for the tough living conditions.

- **What kinds of stresses or strains might a person aboard a drillship for nearly two months experience?**

"I'm always humbled when I come to a port and see a ship waiting and know I get to go out on it," Fisher says. "There are people from all different countries doing all different kinds of research. There's nothing like it in the world."

After Reading:

- Based on the information in the article, draw a diagram of what you think the boat is like. Be sure to label important parts of the ship. For additional information about the ship, see *www-odp.tamu.edu/shipinfo.html* (*Ocean Drilling Program, Texas A&M University*).

- Name at least four different uses for the samples that this research ship is collecting.

- Why is it important to drill into Earth's crust not only on land but also in the middle of the ocean?

- Imagine that you had a sample of the rock that scientists gather in the ocean drilling project. What would you want to study in the sample? Design an experiment that you might perform.

- Where do you think scientists get money for projects like the one described in the article? For additional information on funding, see *www.geo.nsf.gov/oce/programs/drilling.htm* (*National Science Foundation*).

- What risks might there be in going on an expedition aboard the *JOIDES Resolution*? What sorts of accidents could happen?

Ocean Avalanche

You've probably heard stories about tragic avalanches that claim the lives of skiers or mountain climbers, but did you know that avalanches can take place even on the floor of the ocean? It's true—and the landslides that happen deep below the surface of the water can have dramatic consequences for those of us living on land, as author Sorcha McDonagh shows in the following article.

—The Editor

Slip Slidin' Away—Under the Sea

by Sorcha McDonagh

An avalanche can send thousands of tons of rock and mud tumbling down a mountainside, wrecking everything in its way: trees, roads, bridges, buildings, and more. Eventually, the motion stops and the dust settles.

It can take much longer for debris to settle when an avalanche happens beneath the ocean. Underwater landslides can keep going and going—even along surfaces that are nearly flat. These huge, rolling masses of clay and silt sometimes wipe out plant and animal life over vast areas of the seafloor.

What keeps ocean avalanches on the move?

Norwegian scientists have used computers to help solve the puzzle. They figure that undersea avalanches travel far and fast because the moving **sediment** rides on a thin layer of water trapped between the sediment and the seafloor. This water layer cuts down the friction, letting the sediment keep sliding for long distances, sometimes at high speed.

Anders Elverhøi of the University of Oslo and his coworkers described their results in January 2004's *Journal of Geophysical Research—Oceans*.

Something similar can happen to cars and trucks in

wet weather. When traveling along a wet road, a car can lose its grip on the asphalt—making the car go into an uncontrollable slide. This loss of traction is known as **hydroplaning**. It's caused by a layer of water between the tire and the road.

Hydroplaning might explain the size and reach of a massive avalanche known as the Storegga slide. It took place in the Norwegian Sea about 8,000 years ago. Enough sediment to make up several mountains broke free in that avalanche, and some of slid nearly 500 kilometers [311 miles].

And, in a 1929 slide just south of Newfoundland, 300 to 700 cubic kilometers [72 to 168 cubic miles] of sediment sped across the seafloor at nearly 80 kilometers [50 km] per hour, snapping several transatlantic communication cables.

Crabs, shrimp, and Nemo, get out of the way! Once an underwater landslide gets going, there's no stopping it until it's moved a long, long way.

Going Deeper:

Perkins, Sid. "Scooting on a Wet Bottom: Some Undersea Landslides Ride a Nearly Frictionless Slick of Water." *Science News* 165 (January 23, 2004): 84. Available online at *http://www.sciencenews.org/20040124/fob7.asp*.

Finding the Lost City

Off the eastern coast of Bermuda in the Caribbean Sea lies a massive array of rocks. It is known to scientists as the Lost City because of its complex spires and steep structures, which make it resemble a thriving metropolis deep beneath the sea. Among the mounds and cracks of the Lost City are undersea vents that spit out warm liquid, and they have been active for tens of thousands of years. As author Emily Sohn explains, studying the vents of the Lost City may provide scientists with valuable knowledge about how life on Earth began.

—The Editor

Undersea Vent System Active for Ages

by Emily Sohn

Deep at the bottom of the Atlantic Ocean, there is a huge and mysterious network of rock structures called the Lost City.

Rock spires on the steep slopes of an undersea mountain stretch as high as 18-story buildings. Cracks in the rocks spit out warm fluids that are full of minerals.

Scientists have recently uncovered new clues about the chemical workings of the Lost City. The research might help explain how life began.

The search for life's beginnings often focuses on bubbling cracks in the seafloor, called hydrothermal vents. Underwater volcanoes heat most vent systems. The Lost City is different. There, chemical reactions between seawater and rocks warm the oozing flow of mineral-rich liquids.

Researchers from Switzerland analyzed sediment from the Lost City, which lies 2,500 km [1,553 miles] east of Bermuda. They found rock deposits on the chimneys that are 25,000 years old. However, white, feathery structures around the vents formed just in the last few decades.

All together, the new data suggests that the Lost City's vent system has been spewing warm fluids for at least 30,000 years.

Tons of tiny microbes live near the vents, happy as clams. Studying them might help explain how the world's first microbes formed.

Finding the Lost City was only the first step. Many mysteries remain!

Going Deeper:

Perkins, Sid. "Long-term Ocean Venting: Seafloor System Has Been Active for Ages." *Science News* **164 (July 26, 2003): 52. Available online at** *http://www.sciencenews.org/20030726/fob3.asp*.

Alvin Explores Undersea

We live in a technologically advanced world, so it's easy to think there is little more to learn about our planet, but it's not true. The vast area under the sea, in particular, remains a mystery, mainly because we have long lacked the kind of equipment capable of exploring the extreme depths of the oceans. That may be changing. As writer Emily Sohn shows in the following article, a sophisticated underwater vehicle—called "Alvin"—has been helping scientists make tremendous progress in learning what lies below the sea. Soon, Alvin will be replaced by an even better undersea explorer.

—The Editor

Explorer of the Extreme Deep

by Emily Sohn

Before Reading:

- **What would you expect to see at the bottom of the ocean?**

- **What kind of vehicle would you use to explore the ocean floor at great depths?**

It's dark at the bottom of the ocean. It's cold down there, too. There's no air to breathe. The water pressure is crushing. There may be creatures that could harm you.

Let's face it: The deep sea can be an unpleasant place.

Nonetheless, the watery depths hold an irresistible allure for many people. Enormous squid mingle with fantastic sponges, glowing shrimp, and fat worms. Black plumes bubbling out of the seafloor might hold the secret to the origins of life on Earth.

Oceans cover more than two-thirds of our planet. Yet, just a small fraction of the underwater world has been explored.

A new project aims to shed additional light on the ocean depths.

Scientists at the Woods Hole Oceanographic Institution (WHOI) in Massachusetts are building an underwater vehicle that will carry explorers as deep as 6,500 meters (21,320 feet). The new machine, known as a manned submersible or human-operated vehicle (HOV), will replace another one named Alvin, which has been operating for 40 years but can go down only 4,500 meters (14,764 feet).

Based on the amazing results of Alvin's explorations, there's plenty more down there to be discovered.

UPGRADE TIME

It's about time for an upgrade, WHOI researchers say.

Alvin has been around for a long time. When it was launched in 1964, the submersible immediately transformed the face of underwater exploration (Figure 4.1). Suddenly, researchers could make repeated visits to great depths—going far, far deeper than scuba divers carrying their own gear.

Since then, Alvin has worked between 200 and 250 days a year, says Daniel Fornari. He's a marine geologist and director of the Deep Ocean Exploration Institute at WHOI. During its lifetime, Alvin has carried some 12,000 people on a total of more than 4,000 dives.

"It's really the only submersible that dives on a regular basis every year," Fornari says. "It makes as many dives as all other deep-diving submersibles in the world put together."

Alvin can't get to the deepest point in the ocean, and the new vehicle won't be able to go there either. This place, the Challenger Deep in the South Pacific, is 10,915 meters (6.8 miles) below sea level. (To get a sense of how deep that is, consider the fact that the tallest point on land, Mount Everest, is 8,850 meters [29,035 feet] high. If you could put the base of the mountain at the bottom of Challenger Deep, there would still be more than a mile of water above the mountain.)

By diving as deep as 6,500 meters [21,326 feet], however, the new HOV will still be able to explore more than 99 percent of Earth's seafloor.

Figure 4.1 Alvin, seen here working underwater, was first launched in 1964 and has made some impressive discoveries.

DEEP VENTS

Alvin has an amazing record of discovery, playing a key role in various important and famous undersea expeditions.

More than 25 years ago, in 1977, scientists using Alvin found deep-sea **hydrothermal vents** in a place called the Galapagos Rift (Figure 4.2).

- **How deep is the deepest part of the ocean?**

Hydrothermal means "hot water." It's a fitting name for the scalding plumes of fluid that gush out of the seafloor in some places deep in the ocean. Temperatures in the plumes can reach 400 degrees Celsius [752°F].

The fluid itself contains a unique mixture of minerals and chemicals that support exotic deep-ocean ecosystems of microbes, tubeworms, giant clams, and white crabs.

Today, all sorts of researchers and explorers wait for years to get time on Alvin, says Blee Williams, who worked as an Alvin pilot for 11 years.

During his 300-plus dives on Alvin, Williams has helped biologists collect worms and sponges, chemists gather rocks, and oceanographers map the seafloor and take water samples, among many other projects.

- **What's a hydrothermal vent?**

Geologists such as Fornari study underwater volcanoes. They look at ocean ridges to understand how the planet's surface has changed over time.

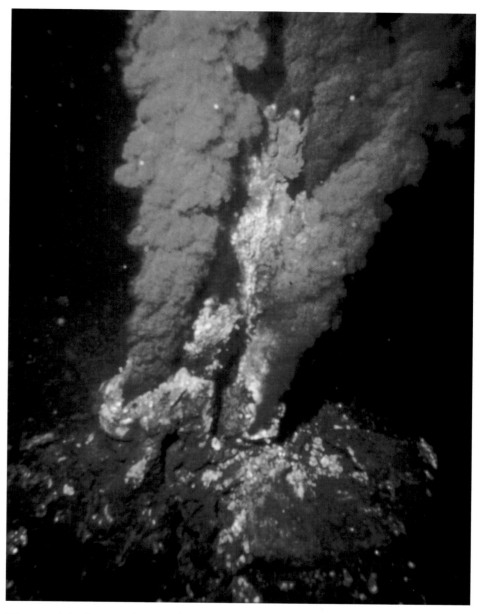

Figure 4.2 Hydrothermal vents like this one are sometimes called "black smokers." They serve as habitats for strange life-forms that thrive on the extreme heat they give off.

In 1986, Alvin provided the first photographs of the steamship *Titanic*, which sank in the North Atlantic after striking an iceberg in 1912.

NEWER, BETTER

A newer, better version of Alvin is bound to reveal even more surprises about a world that is still full of mysteries, Fornari says.

> • **Name two discoveries that Alvin was responsible for.**

It might also make the job of exploration a little easier. "We take so much for granted on land," Fornari says. "We can walk around and see with our eyes how big things are. We can see colors, special arrangements. Once you go under the surface of the ocean, you have to work really hard to get the same kinds of information."

Size-wise, the new HOV will be similar to Alvin. It'll be about 27 feet [8 meters] long, roughly the size of a small school bus. The sitting area inside will be a small sphere, about 6 feet [2 meters] wide. Like Alvin, it'll carry a pilot and two passengers. It will be just as maneuverable.

In most other ways, the new, still-unnamed sub will feature plenty of welcome improvements. It'll give passengers more opportunities to enjoy the view, for one thing. Alvin has only three windows, called view ports. The new vehicle will have five, with more overlap so that the passengers and the pilot can see the same things.

Power and speed will also get major boosts. Alvin can go up and down at a rate of 30 meters [98 feet] every second, and its maximum speed is 2 knots (about 2.3 miles per hour). The new sub will be able to ascend and descend at 44 meters [144 feet] per second. It'll reach speeds of 3 knots, or 3.5 miles per hour.

Getting to the bottom faster and moving around more quickly will allow researchers to make the most of their limited time underwater. A typical dive lasts just nine hours. After that, the sub has to come up to a support ship for maintenance and repairs.

Going super-deep comes with added challenges. To withstand the water pressure that comes with 2,000 extra meters [6,562 feet] of depth, the new vehicle will have a thicker titanium shell and heartier equipment. It'll carry the latest and greatest cameras and other technology for collecting data.

EXCITING POSSIBILITIES

Scientists are excited about the possibilities that the new Alvin will offer.

"It will open up new horizons," Fornari says. "It'll give us a much better understanding of features and

- In what ways will the new deep-sea vehicle be better than Alvin?

areas that we previously have not been able to go to."

It should be an exciting ride for the people who get to experience the new sub, too.

Dive after dive on Alvin, Williams says, he saw scientists go speechless at the wonders of being on the other side of the fishbowl. There are few words to express how amazing the view is at the bottom of the sea, he says.

For most of his passengers, it was a lifetime of dreams come true. One of his favorite dives involved astronaut Kathy Sullivan. "She was the first woman to walk in outer space," Williams says. "She was still like a kid when she went to the bottom of the ocean."

Ready to sign up for classes to become a submersible pilot?

Williams recommends a healthy interest in all sorts of science and a willingness to learn new things all the time. No two days with Alvin were ever the same, he says.

Being good with tools and machinery is also important, Williams adds. Alvin required a large amount of daily maintenance, which included completely taking it apart and rebuilding it periodically.

"As an engineer for Alvin," Williams says, "you never knew how you were going to be challenged."

To be ready in time to ride in the shiny new vehicle, you'll probably want to start studying right away. It's set to launch in 2008.

After Reading:

• Use the information in the article to draw a picture of Alvin. Label its parts. For additional information, see *www.whoi.edu/marops/vehicles/alvin/alvin_photos.html* (*Woods Hole Oceanographic Institution*).

• Alvin's successor doesn't yet have a name. What would you name the new vehicle? Why?

• Compare and contrast deep-sea exploration to space exploration.

• What kind of equipment for research would you want on a trip in Alvin? Come up with three to five things you would need to have with you. Explain why you would need each item.

• Why do you think that engineers can now build a better vehicle for undersea exploration than they could in the 1960s? Come up with examples of technological improvements that have occurred that would benefit this form of exploration.

• What sorts of animals live near hydrothermal vents? What makes them different from most other sea creatures? See *www.onr.navy.mil/focus/ocean/habitats/vents2.htm* (*Office of Naval Research*).

• Compare what a geologist aboard Alvin might look for to what a marine biologist might try to observe. Come up with a question that each might ask about the ocean depths.

Glossary

breakwaters: An offshore structure (like a wall) that protects a beach from ocean waves.

crater: Bowl-shaped depression around the mouth of a volcano.

deuterium: An isotope of hydrogen that has one proton and one neutron and has twice the mass of ordinary hydrogen.

diurnal temperature range (DTR): The difference between temperatures during the day and at night.

drought: A period of prolonged dryness.

El Niño: Flow of unusually warm surface waters from the Pacific Ocean toward the coast of South America that causes disturbances in regional and global weather patterns.

fault lines: Fractures in the crust of the Earth.

fossil fuels: Coal, oil, or natural gas produced in the Earth from the remains of plants or animals.

geology: The study of the history of the Earth and its living things, as recorded in rocks.

gravity: Force of attraction between celestial objects.

harmonic tremor: Continuous rhythmic earthquakes in the Earth's lithosphere.

hurricane: A tropical cyclone with winds of at least 74 miles (119 km) per hour.

hydroplaning: Skimming along a wet surface.

hydrothermal vents: Crack in the ocean floor from which super-heated water comes out.

incubators: Devices that provide artificially controlled environmental conditions.

La Niña: A recurring upwelling of unusually cold water along the coast of South America that often follows El Niño and causes disturbances in weather patterns.

lava dome: Mound-shaped growth formed by the flow of lava from an erupting volcano.

magma: Molten rock material inside the Earth that forms igneous rock when it cools.

mantle: The part of the Earth that lies above the central core and below the crust.

meteorology: The study of weather and climate change.

microbes: Living organisms that are too small to be seen without the aid of a microscope.

microbiologists: Scientists who study microscopic organisms.

photosynthesis: The process of plant respiration in which carbon dioxide is taken in, converted, and released as oxygen.

plates: Tectonic plates; large pieces of the Earth's crust that move and collide, forming mountains and other changes on the surface of the planet.

P waves: Pressure waves; waves caused by variations in pressure.

sediment: The solid matter that settles to the bottom of liquid.

seismologist: A scientist who studies earthquakes.

S waves: A wave caused by a cut in an elastic medium; for example, earthquakes produce S waves because they cause tears in the Earth.

tsunami: A huge sea wave caused by an underground earthquake or volcanic eruption.

typhoons: Hurricanes that occur in the Philippines or China Sea.

Books

Barnard, Bryn. *Dangerous Planet: Natural Disasters That Changed History*. New York: Crown Publishers/ Random House, 2003.

Gold, Susan Dudley. *Blame It on El Niño*. New York: Raintree Steck-Vaughn, 1999.

Kovacs, Deborah. *Dive to the Deep Ocean*. New York: Raintree Steck-Vaughn, 2000.

Silverstein, Alvin, Laura Silverstein Nunn, and Virginia Silverstein. *Plate Tectonics*. Minneapolis: Twenty-First Century Books/Millbrook Press, 1998.

Wade, Mary Dodson. *Tsunami: Monster Waves*. Berkeley Heights, NJ: Enslow Publishers, 2002.

Vogel, Carole Garbuny. *Nature's Fury: Eyewitness Reports of Natural Disasters*. New York: Scholastic, 2000.

Websites

Hurricanes
http://www.fema.gov/kids/h urr.htm

Integrated Ocean Drilling Program
http://www.oceandrilling.org/

Mount St. Helens VolcanoCam
http://www.fs.fed.us/gpnf/volcanocams/msh/

National Drought Mitigation Center
http://www.drought.unl.edu/

National Hurricane Center
http://www.nhc.noaa.gov/index.shtml

National Oceanic and Atmospheric Administration
http://hurricanes.noaa.gov/prepare/structure.htm

Waves of Destruction: Tsunamis
http://www.pbs.org/wnet/savageearth/tsunami/
index.html

Trademarks

Coke is a registered trademark of the Coca-Cola Company; Frisbee is a registered trademark of Wham-O Inc.; iPod is a registered trademark of Apple Computer, Inc.; Sour Patch Kids is a registered trademark of Cadbury Adams Canada Inc.

Index

118

Picture Credits

page:

3: Eric Nguyen/Jim Reed Photography/CORBIS
9: Reuters/CORBIS
22: David Ball/CORBIS
33: BEAWIHARTA/Reuters/CORBIS
48: Joseph Sohm/Chromo Sohm Inc./CORBIS
49: Gary Koellhoffer
52: © Corel Corporation
59: U.S. Geological Service
69: U.S. Geological Service
80: Ken Lucas/Visuals Unlimited
85: © Corel Corporation
105: Ralph White/CORBIS
107: Science VU/Visuals Unlimited

EMILY SOHN is a freelance journalist, based in Minneapolis. She covers mostly science and health for national magazines, including *U.S. News & World Report*, *Health*, *Smithsonian*, and *Science News*. Emily divides her time between writing for kids and writing for adults, and assignments have sent her to countries around the world, including Cuba, Peru, and Sweden. When she's not working, Emily spends most of her time rock climbing, camping, swimming, exploring, and pursuing adventures outdoors.

TARA KOELLHOFFER earned her degree in political science and history from Rutgers University. Today, she is a freelance writer and editor with ten years of experience working on nonfiction books for young adults, covering topics that range from social studies and biography to health and science. She has edited hundreds of books and teaching materials, including a history of Italy published by Greenhaven Press. She lives in Pennsylvania with her husband, Gary, and their dog and cat.